AFFILIATE MARKETING

FOR OLD GEEZERS AND HIGH SCHOOL KIDS

[Darwin Dallyn]

Table of Contents

INTRODUCTION

Welcome to "Affiliate Marketing: For Old Geezers and High School Kids." If you've picked up this book, you've probably wondered if the affiliate marketing world is right for you. Maybe you're a retiree looking to add excitement and income to your golden years or a high schooler eager to step into the entrepreneurial arena. This tutorial is intended to demystify the notion of affiliate marketing and empower you to develop a profitable company, regardless of whatever category you fall into.

So, what exactly is affiliate marketing, and why should you be concerned? Affiliate marketing, in its most basic form, is a means of earning a commission by advertising other people's or businesses' products. You find a product you like, promote it to others, and profit from each sale you make. It's a powerful way to generate online income, and the beauty of it is that you don't have to create your product to start making money.

This book aims to be the definitive guide to affiliate marketing, whether you're a complete newbie or have some experience in this field. We'll begin with a solid foundation by unpacking the basics in Chapter 1, "Understanding Affiliate Marketing." Here, we delve into the history, workings, benefits, and challenges of affiliate marketing. Plus, we'll guide you in finding a niche that suits your interest and expertise.

The next chapters guide you through setting up your affiliate marketing business, from choosing the right programs to building your online presence and marketing platform. You'll learn how to create engaging content, build an engaged audience, and leverage various tools such as social media, email marketing, and webinars to boost your sales. In Chapter 4, we dive into advanced techniques such as influencer marketing, video marketing, paid advertising, and cross-promotions. These techniques can amplify your earning potential and set you apart.

Then, we take a specialized focus on two distinct groups: old geezers and high school kids. Although affiliate marketing can be profitable for anyone, these two groups face unique challenges and opportunities. You'll learn how to choose products that resonate with your age group, navigate legal and parental issues (for the high schoolers), and leverage your unique strengths. As your business grows, you'll need to think about scaling up. Chapter 7 gives practical advice on automation, outsourcing, expanding your product portfolio, and diversifying your income streams. However, growth comes with challenges, which we address in Chapter 8. From dealing with changes in affiliate programs to maintaining motivation, we've got you covered.

We also ensure you understand the legal and ethical implications of affiliate marketing. We explore FTC guidelines, cookie laws, and transparency requirements, to name a few. Finally, we look towards the future of affiliate marketing, highlighting industry trends, new technologies, and changes in consumer behavior you'll need to anticipate.

This book is a comprehensive blueprint for starting and scaling your affiliate marketing business, regardless of age or experience. As we embark on this journey together, keep an open mind, be ready to learn, and most importantly, take action on what you learn. So, are you ready to enter the fascinating affiliate marketing world and start creating your income streams? If so, let's get started.

CHAPTER-1: UNDERSTANDING AFFILIATE MARKETING

Welcome to the first step of your affiliate marketing journey. In this chapter, we will help you understand the basics of affiliate marketing, its history, how it works, its benefits and challenges, and how to find your niche.

What Is Affiliate Marketing?

Affiliate marketing is a performance-based business strategy in which an affiliate is compensated for selling the items of another person or company. The affiliate discovers a product they like, promotes it, and earns a portion of the sale price.

This marketing method connects marketers with customers. It is a method for businesses to enhance sales by allowing people with an audience - affiliates - to advertise their products and services. Affiliates can make money by marketing relevant items and services to their audience.

Affiliate marketing is a performance-based digital marketing technique that allows firms to reach a wider audience and increase sales by using a network of partners or 'affiliates.' These affiliates, individuals, or other businesses earn a commission by promoting the company's products or services to their audience. It's a partnership where the company provides affiliates with unique links or promotional codes. These trackable tools allow the company to monitor which affiliate drives sales. In return, the affiliate earns a commission for every purchase made through their link or using their code.

The process begins when the affiliate finds a product they like or feel their audience would be interested in and then promotes it. This promotion can happen through various channels such as blogs, YouTube videos, email marketing, social media posts, or any other platform where the affiliate has an audience. To assist the affiliate in creating interesting content around the product or service, the firm provides promotional tools like banners, social network postings, and email templates. When members of the affiliate's audience click on the provided link and make a purchase, the sale is attributed to that particular affiliate based on the unique tracking code embedded in the link, and they receive a pre-agreed commission for driving that sale.

The attractive aspect of affiliate marketing is that it's a win-win scenario for both parties. Affiliates can make cash without generating a product, while companies profit from greater visibility and sales. Many firms like this marketing technique because it is cost-effective, as they only pay for conversions rather than impressions or clicks, decreasing their risk dramatically. Affiliate marketing is a popular and efficient digital marketing approach that helps firms and affiliates while offering value to end users.

A Brief History Of Affiliate Marketing

Revenue sharing—paying commission for referred business—was practiced long before the internet. However, the rise of the internet and e-commerce platforms took it to a new level.

Amazon launched one of the first online affiliate programs, "Amazon Associates," 1996. This program allowed associates to place banner or text links on their site for

Amazon products and earn referral fees when customers clicked through them and bought products from Amazon. This concept has since been adopted by thousands of businesses, paving the way for affiliate marketing as we know it today.

Affiliate marketing, an integral facet of digital marketing today, traces its roots back to the mid-1990s, right after the advent of the World Wide Web. As e-commerce began flourishing, William J. Tobin, the founder of PC Flowers & Gifts, conceived and implemented the affiliate marketing business model. Tobin applied for a patent in 1989 for the concept, which was granted in 1996. His model provided a system where partner websites, termed 'affiliates,' promoted PC Flowers & Gifts products in exchange for a share of the profits.

In 1996, Amazon adopted a similar approach, launching the Amazon Associates program, which enabled website owners, bloggers, and influencers to earn a commission by promoting Amazon's products. The success of the Amazon Associates program became a blueprint for many companies, bolstering the growth of affiliate marketing exponentially.

The turn of the millennium saw further advancements, with affiliate networks like Commission Junction and ClickBank emerging as intermediaries between merchants and affiliates. These networks simplified the process by managing the relationship, tracking and reporting data, and ensuring timely payment of commissions.

The rise of blogging and social media in the 2000s provided affiliates with new channels for promotion, dramatically transforming the landscape of affiliate marketing. Affiliate marketing became more accessible and profitable with improved tracking systems, better commission structures, and a wider range of products to promote.

By the 2010s, with the widespread penetration of smartphones and high-speed internet, the market for affiliate marketing had grown into a multi-billion dollar industry. Innovations such as automated affiliate marketing software and more sophisticated data analytics tools made it possible to track affiliate performance with greater precision, allowing for more effective strategies and better revenue generation.

As of today, affiliate marketing has evolved into a complex yet rewarding digital marketing strategy that relies on a symbiotic relationship between advertisers, affiliates, and consumers. It's a sector expected to develop more, thanks to technical improvements and trends in customer behavior toward online purchasing.

How Does Affiliate Marketing Work?

Affiliate marketing works through a chain of events. First, an affiliate joins an affiliate program, where they're given a unique affiliate link. This link is trackable and maintains track of everyone the affiliate refers to on the merchant's website.

A cookie is stored on their device when a potential customer clicks the link. This cookie guarantees the affiliate receives credit for the referral transaction, even if it happens days or weeks later. If the customer purchases a product, the merchant checks the sale, approves it, and gives a commission to the affiliate.

Benefits And Challenges Of Affiliate Marketing

Affiliate marketing comes with several benefits. For one, it's a low-cost business venture. You don't need to create a product or handle inventory, shipping, and customer service. You also have the freedom to work from anywhere and at any time. Moreover, the earning potential is virtually limitless, depending on your marketing skills and the audience reach.

However, like any business model, it also comes with challenges. It requires time, effort, and patience, especially in the beginning when you are building your audience. It may also take a while before you start seeing significant earnings. The fluctuation in income and competition are other common challenges you might face.

Finding Your Niche In Affiliate Marketing

Your niche should be something you are genuinely interested in or passionate about. It should also have a good amount of potential customers and affiliate products that you can promote.

Start by brainstorming topics you're passionate about, have expertise in, or are interested in learning more about. Then, validate your ideas by researching the competition, potential audience, and availability of affiliate products. The goal is to find a niche where you can provide value and build your authority.

At the end of this chapter, you should understand what affiliate marketing is, its history, how it works, its benefits and challenges, and how to find your niche. This information will serve as the foundation for the next chapters, where we will establish an affiliate marketing firm. So buckle up and prepare to discover more.

CHAPTER-2: GETTING STARTED IN AFFILIATE MARKETING

Now that we've established what affiliate marketing is and its benefits and challenges let's move on to the practical aspects of setting up your affiliate marketing business. This chapter covers setting up your online presence, choosing the right affiliate programs, creating your marketing strategy, and understanding the legal and ethical considerations.

Setting Up Your Online Presence

Your online presence is the platform through which you'll promote your affiliate products. This might be in the shape of a blog, a website, a YouTube channel, or a social media account. Your abilities and interests heavily influence the decision and where your target audience spends most of their online time.

Starting with a blog or website is often a fantastic place to start, especially if you like writing. Choose a domain name that corresponds to your specialty and a hosting provider. To attract organic visitors, make sure your website is properly built, easy to use, and search engine optimized.

Choosing The Right Affiliate Programs

There are countless affiliate programs, and choosing the right ones is crucial. Consider factors such as the relevance of the products to your audience, the commission structure, the company's reputation, and the support offered by the program. Some popular affiliate networks that connect affiliates with multiple programs include Amazon Associates, ShareASale, and ClickBank.

Creating Your Affiliate Marketing Strategy

Your affiliate marketing strategy outlines how you'll promote the affiliate products. It includes understanding your audience, the types of content you'll create, your traffic generation strategies, and your plan for converting visitors into customers.

Consider what difficulties your target market is attempting to address and how the solutions you offer may assist them. Create material that will educate, entertain, and persuade your target audience about these items. Search engine optimization (SEO), email marketing, social media marketing, and paid advertising might all be part of your traffic creation strategy.

Legal And Ethical Considerations In Affiliate Marketing

Being transparent about your affiliate relationships is not only ethical but it's also required by law in many regions. When promoting affiliate products, disclose this to your audience. For instance, the Federal Trade Commission requires affiliates to disclose their affiliate relationships clearly and conspicuously on their websites in the United States.

Tracking And Analyzing Your Affiliate Marketing Performance

Lastly, it's important to track your affiliate marketing performance. This includes monitoring the number of clicks on your affiliate links, conversions (sales made), and the income generated. Most affiliate networks offer a dashboard where you may examine these stats.

Analyzing your performance helps you understand what's working and what's not so that you can optimize your strategy. It can also help you identify the most popular products with your audience and potentially uncover new opportunities.

Starting your affiliate marketing business can seem daunting, but it's completely manageable with the right approach and tools. Remember, the journey to a successful affiliate marketing business is a marathon, not a sprint. Be patient, keep learning, and stay consistent; your efforts will pay off in the long run.

CHAPTER-3: BUILDING YOUR AFFILIATE MARKETING PLATFORM

In the previous chapter, we laid out the steps to get started in affiliate marketing. Now, it's time to build upon those initial foundations. This chapter will delve into the practicalities of building your affiliate marketing platform, including creating a blog or website, content creation, SEO, audience building, social media, and email marketing.

Creating A Blog Or Website For Affiliate Marketing

The cornerstone of your affiliate marketing platform will often be a blog or a website. It is your digital real estate where you will provide valuable content, build your audience, and promote your affiliate products. Use platforms like WordPress or Wix to build your website. The website is visually appealing, user-friendly, and mobile-friendly, with a clear call-to-action (CTA) instructing your audience on what to do next.

Content Creation And Seo For Affiliate Marketing

Content is king in affiliate marketing. It's how you communicate with your audience, provide value, build trust, and promote your affiliate products. The type of content you create can range from blog posts, reviews, tutorials, videos, and infographics to podcasts. Regardless of the format, ensure your content is high-quality, relevant, engaging, and offers value to your audience.

Optimize your content for search engines to generate organic visitors to your site. This is where SEO comes into play. Use keywords your audience is searching for, include internal and external links, and write compelling meta descriptions. Tools like Google's Keyword Planner, SEMrush, or Yoast SEO can help your SEO efforts.

Building An Engaged Audience And Community

Without an audience, your affiliate marketing efforts will fall flat. Start by identifying your target audience — who they are, what they need, their challenges, and how you can help them. Use your content to attract them, then engage them by encouraging comments, asking for feedback, and responding to their inquiries.

Building a community around your brand makes your audience feel valued and fosters loyalty. It also enhances your credibility and increases the likelihood of your audience purchasing the products you recommend.

Utilizing Social Media For Affiliate Marketing

Social media platforms are powerful tools for affiliate marketers. They provide a means of reaching a broader audience, engaging with them, and driving traffic to your website. The key to social media success is to select sites where your target audience spends their time, whether it's Instagram, Facebook, Twitter, Pinterest, or LinkedIn.

Post regularly, engage with your followers, use compelling visuals, and include affiliate links where appropriate. However, remember to disclose your affiliate relationships to comply with the platform's and FTC's rules.

Email Marketing And Affiliate Promotions

Another critical component of a good affiliate marketing network is email marketing. It allows you to engage with your audience directly, create relationships, and promote your affiliate items.

Start by offering something of value in exchange for your website visitors' email addresses, such as a free ebook, a course, or a newsletter. Once you've built your email list, send regular emails that offer value and occasionally promote your affiliate products. Remember that your focus should be on providing value, not just selling.

Building a robust affiliate marketing platform is a process. It takes perseverance, patience, and a desire to learn and adapt. However, your efforts to create quality content, engage with your audience, and leverage SEO, social media, and email marketing will pay off in the long run with increased traffic, audience trust, and affiliate sales.

CHAPTER-4: ADVANCED AFFILIATE MARKETING TECHNIQUES

At this point, you've got a strong foundation for your affiliate marketing platform. However, the affiliate marketing world isn't static, and as your business grows, you'll want to expand your toolkit and employ advanced techniques. This chapter will explore leveraging influencer marketing, video marketing, webinars, paid advertising, and cross-promotions.

Leveraging Influencer Marketing In Affiliate Campaigns

Influencer marketing involves partnering with influential people in your niche to promote your affiliate products. These influencers have a large following that trusts their recommendations, and leveraging their influence can significantly boost your affiliate sales.

To begin, identify influencers in your niche who align with your business. You can contact them directly or use platforms like Instagram, TikTok, or YouTube. Propose a partnership where they promote your affiliate products to their followers.

Using Youtube And Video Marketing For Affiliates

Video content is incredibly engaging and can dramatically enhance your affiliate marketing efforts. Platforms like YouTube allow you to create product reviews, tutorials, unboxing videos, and more centered around your affiliate products.

When creating video content, ensure it's high-quality, engaging, and provides value. Include a clear call to action directing viewers to your affiliate products, and remember to disclose your affiliate links.

Harnessing The Power Of Webinars In Affiliate Sales

Webinars are live, interactive sessions where you provide valuable content to your audience and promote your affiliate products. They're an excellent platform for demonstrating the use of a product, addressing frequently asked questions, and making a more personalized sales pitch.

Hosting a webinar doesn't require a huge budget. With software like Zoom or WebinarJam, you can easily connect with your audience, share your knowledge, and promote your affiliate products in a real-time, interactive setting.

Mastering Paid Advertising For Affiliate Success

Paid advertising can also boost your affiliate marketing efforts. Platforms such as Google and Facebook Ads enable you to develop customized ad campaigns that lead visitors to your affiliate offers.

Paid advertising requires a budget, and there's a learning curve involved in creating effective campaigns. However, it can significantly increase your reach and affiliate sales.

Implementing Cross-Promotions And Joint Ventures

Cross-promotions involve partnering with other affiliates or product owners to promote each other's products. This strategy can help you reach a wider audience, increase your credibility, and boost affiliate sales.

Joint ventures are similar to cross-promotions but usually involve a closer collaboration, such as creating a product. These partnerships can be lucrative but require high trust and coordination between parties.

Implementing advanced affiliate marketing techniques can greatly enhance your reach and sales. However, these techniques often require more time, effort, and investment, so it's essential to carefully plan and monitor your efforts to ensure a positive return on investment. Remember, the goal isn't to use all techniques but to find those that work best for your business and audience.

CHAPTER-5: MONETIZING AFFILIATE MARKETING FOR OLD GEEZERS

Age should never be a barrier to success, and in affiliate marketing, it can be an advantage. In this chapter, we'll explore how older adults, affectionately referred to as "Old Geezers," can leverage their life experiences, nostalgia, and niche markets to succeed in affiliate marketing.

Choosing Products Relevant To The Older Audience

One of the advantages of being an older affiliate marketer is that you understand your peers' needs, preferences, and challenges. Use this understanding to choose affiliate products relevant to the older audience. This could range from health and wellness products, hobbies and crafts, travel, and retirement planning to tech gadgets designed for seniors.

Connecting With Senior-Focused Affiliate Programs

Several affiliate programs cater specifically to the older demographic. These programs offer products and services designed to meet seniors' needs. Promoting such products can create a highly targeted and effective affiliate marketing business that resonates with your audience.

Overcoming Age-Related Challenges In Affiliate Marketing

While age brings wisdom and experience, it can also bring challenges. For instance, some older adults may not be as tech-savvy as their younger counterparts. Don't let this deter you. Numerous resources available, both online and offline, can help you build your tech skills.

Another potential challenge is the misconception that affiliate marketing is for the younger generation. This couldn't be further from the truth. Affiliate marketing is about connecting people with products they need, which can be done effectively by people of all ages.

Leveraging Life Experience For Authentic Affiliate Promotions

Your life experience is a goldmine in affiliate marketing. It gives you authenticity, a highly valued quality in this field. Use your experiences to create genuine, relatable, and engaging content. Share your stories, insights, and lessons learned. This can help your audience trust you and make your affiliate marketing more appealing.

Tapping Into Nostalgia And Niche Markets For Old Geezers

Nostalgia marketing is a powerful strategy that can help you connect with your audience emotionally. Promoting products that bring back fond memories can evoke emotions that drive purchasing decisions.

Similarly, tapping into niche markets can be highly profitable. Whether it's vintage collectibles, classic cars, gardening, or genealogy, find a niche that aligns with your interests and those of your peers.

Being an older affiliate marketer can be a unique advantage. Your life experiences, demographic analysis, and ability to tap into nostalgia and specialized markets may all help you develop a popular and profitable affiliate marketing organization.

CHAPTER-6: MONETIZING AFFILIATE MARKETING FOR HIGH SCHOOL KIDS

This chapter is for you if you're a high school student eager to dive into the affiliate marketing world. Although you're young, don't underestimate the potential you hold. Here, we will explore the unique opportunities available to high school affiliates, alongside legal and parental considerations, content creation for young audiences, collaboration with youth-centric brands, and balancing school life with affiliate marketing.

Understanding The Unique Opportunities For High School Affiliates

As a high school affiliate marketer, you bring a fresh perspective. You have a pulse on trends and preferences of your age group that many older marketers may also not understand. Utilize this knowledge to promote products that appeal to your peers, from trending fashion and tech gadgets to study aids and online games.

Navigating Legal And Parental Consent Issues

Before you begin your affiliate marketing adventure, you must first grasp the legal consequences. For instance, you may need parental consent to sign up for affiliate programs if you're under 18. Furthermore, any income you earn must be reported for tax purposes. Discuss your plans with a trusted adult to ensure you know and can navigate any potential legal hurdles.

Creating Content That Appeals To Young Audiences

Your peers are your primary audience, so create content that speaks to them. You might consider using platforms popular among your age group, such as TikTok or Instagram, and produce content formats that your peers enjoy, such as video content or interactive polls. Keep your content authentic, relatable, and fun. Remember to respect the rules of any platform you use and always disclose affiliate links.

Collaborating With Youth-Centric Brands And Programs

Working with brands and programs that target young people can enhance your affiliate marketing success. These brands are more likely to appreciate your understanding of the youth market and may offer products your peers are more interested in. Research and connect with youth-centric brands that align with your interests and audience.

Balancing School, Life, And Affiliate Marketing Success

While affiliate marketing can be exciting and lucrative, maintaining balance is essential. School should remain a priority, and ensure you leave time for relaxation and social activities. Effective time management is key to juggling these different elements of your life.

High school students can succeed in affiliate marketing thanks to their unique understanding of youth trends and the digital landscape. You can kick-start your affiliate marketing journey while still in school by understanding your audience, creating engaging content, working with relevant brands, navigating legalities, and maintaining a healthy balance.

CHAPTER-7: SCALING UP YOUR AFFILIATE MARKETING BUSINESS

After establishing a solid affiliate marketing foundation, the next step is to scale your operations. Scaling involves growing your business while maintaining or improving efficiency and effectiveness. This chapter explores automation and outsourcing, expanding your product portfolio, diversifying income streams, building long-term affiliate relationships, and staying ahead of market trends.

Automation And Outsourcing For Affiliate Marketers

As your business grows, manual tasks can become overwhelming. Automation tools can help manage these tasks efficiently. For example, email automation tools can help manage your email campaigns, while social media automation tools can schedule posts in advance.

Outsourcing is another viable option. Consider hiring freelancers or virtual assistants for content creation, graphic design, and administrative tasks.

Expanding Your Affiliate Product Portfolio

Adding more products to your affiliate marketing mix can diversify your income and reduce risk. When selecting new products, consider relevance to your audience, product quality, and the reputation of the product creator.

Don't just add products for the sake of it. Carefully consider how each product fits into your overall strategy and how it will provide value to your audience.

Diversifying Income Streams In Affiliate Marketing

While expanding your product portfolio is one form of diversification, other ways exist to create multiple income streams. For instance, you can earn income from display ads on your blog, sponsorships, or offering paid online courses or consulting services related to your niche.

Remember, diversification isn't just about creating multiple income streams. It's about creating multiple, reliable income streams that align with your brand and provide value to your audience.

Building Long-Term Relationships With Affiliate Partners

Successful affiliate marketing isn't just about making quick sales. It's about building long-term relationships with your affiliate partners. Regularly communicate with your partners, provide feedback, and discuss ways to improve your promotional efforts. Long-term relationships can lead to higher commission rates, exclusive deals, and other benefits.

Keeping Ahead of Competitors and Market Trends

Affiliate marketing is a dynamic industry, and trends can change quickly. It will help to stay abreast of market trends, consumer behavior, and your competitors' actions to stay competitive. This knowledge will help you adapt your strategy, experiment with new techniques, and maintain your edge.

Scaling your affiliate marketing business requires careful planning and execution. You can grow your business while maximizing efficiency by automating tasks, outsourcing work, diversifying income streams, expanding your product portfolio, and building solid relationships. Stay flexible, adapt to changing market trends, and always keep the needs of your audience at the forefront.

CHAPTER-8: OVERCOMING CHALLENGES AND ROADBLOCKS

As with any entrepreneurial venture, affiliate marketing comes with its fair share of challenges and roadblocks. From dealing with program changes and customer complaints to maintaining motivation amid challenges, this chapter will provide strategies for effectively managing these hurdles.

Dealing With Affiliate Program Changes And Closures

Affiliate programs may change their terms or even close without warning, disrupting your income stream. To mitigate this, diversify your affiliate programs to ensure you're not overly reliant on one. Keep abreast of news about your affiliate programs, so you can anticipate changes and adapt accordingly.

Managing Refunds, Chargebacks, And Customer Complaints

Refunds and chargebacks can eat your profits, while customer complaints tarnish your reputation. Choose high-quality products to promote, provide honest and comprehensive product reviews, and promptly address customer complaints to reduce these risks.

Handling Seo And Algorithm Changes Affecting Your Affiliate Site

Search engine algorithms constantly change, affecting your website's visibility. Stay updated on SEO best practices and regularly optimize your site. Remember, good SEO isn't just about keywords; it's about providing valuable, user-friendly content.

Coping With Burnout And Maintaining Motivation

Running an affiliate marketing business can lead to burnout, especially if you do it alongside a full-time job or study. Take frequent pauses, set reasonable goals, and remember to enjoy your accomplishments, no matter how minor they may appear.

Learning From Failures And Turning Them Into Success

Failure is a part of the entrepreneurial journey. Don't let it discourage you. Instead, treat each failure as a learning opportunity. Analyze what went wrong, make necessary adjustments, and keep moving forward.

Overcoming challenges in affiliate marketing requires resilience, flexibility, and a positive mindset. Keep your end goals in sight, and remember that every successful affiliate marketer has faced and overcome these same challenges. It's part of the journey to success.

CHAPTER-9: LEGAL AND ETHICAL CONSIDERATIONS IN AFFILIATE MARKETING

Like any other business, affiliate marketing comes with its legal and ethical obligations. Understanding these aspects is crucial to building trust with your audience, maintaining good relationships with your affiliate partners, and avoiding legal complications. This chapter will guide you through FTC guidelines, cookie laws and privacy policies, plagiarism and copyright issues, ethical practices, and transparency.

Ftc Guidelines For Affiliate Marketers

Affiliate marketers are obligated by the Federal Trade Commission (FTC) to disclose their ties with affiliate partners. If you're promoting and earning a commission from a product, you must clearly state this in your promotional content. Not complying with these guidelines can lead to hefty fines.

Understanding Cookie Laws And Privacy Policies

If you're using cookies on your website, you must inform your visitors and obtain their consent, especially if you have visitors from the European Union. Your website also needs a privacy policy detailing how you collect, use, and store user data.

Dealing With Plagiarism And Copyright Infringement

Using someone else's content without permission can result in copyright infringement. Always create original content or obtain permission to use others' materials. Also, protect your content from being used without your consent.

Ethical Affiliate Marketing Practices And Transparency

Ethics and transparency are crucial in affiliate marketing. Promote products that you genuinely believe in and provide honest reviews. Don't deceive your audience for the sake of earning a commission. Building trust with your audience is paramount and will lead to long-term success.

Building Trust With Your Audience And Affiliate Partners

Maintain open communication with your audience and affiliate partners. Keep your audience informed about your affiliate relationships and respect their data privacy. Treat your affiliate partners fairly, inform them of your marketing strategies, and promptly address any issues.

Understanding and complying with the legal and ethical considerations in affiliate marketing are non-negotiables. These practices keep you out of legal trouble and help build trust and credibility with your audience and partners, which are vital for long-term success in the field.

CHAPTER-10: THE FUTURE OF AFFILIATE MARKETING

Affiliate marketing is not a stagnant industry. The strategies that worked a decade ago might not bring the same results today. It's crucial to keep abreast of evolving industry trends, adapt to new technologies, understand changing consumer behaviors, explore global opportunities, and continually refine your affiliate marketing strategy.

Predictions And Trends For The Affiliate Marketing Industry

While it's hard to predict the future with certainty, we can anticipate that e-commerce and affiliate marketing will continue to grow as more consumers and businesses shift online. Trends such as personalized marketing, voice search, AI, machine learning, and the continued rise of social media influencers are likely to shape the affiliate marketing landscape.

Embracing New Technologies And Platforms

Technological innovations like AI and blockchain could revolutionize affiliate marketing. For example, AI can help improve product recommendations and customer service, while blockchain can offer more transaction transparency. New social media platforms and apps may also provide fresh opportunities for affiliate promotion.

Adapting To Changing Consumer Behavior

As consumers become more tech-savvy, they demand more personalized, authentic, and value-driven interactions with brands. Affiliate marketers who can adapt to these changing preferences and behaviors will stand out. For example, instead of merely promoting a product, consider providing comprehensive reviews, tutorials, and valuable content related to the product.

Global Opportunities In Affiliate Marketing

As the internet bridges geographical boundaries, affiliate marketers are no longer restricted to their home country. Opportunities exist to partner with international brands, target foreign audiences, and promote products globally. However, when exploring these opportunities, be aware of cultural differences, language barriers, and local regulations.

Evolving Your Affiliate Marketing Strategy For The Future

As the industry evolves, so should your affiliate marketing strategy. Keep learning, testing new strategies, and refining your approach based on your results. Remain flexible and adaptable, and stay tuned to industry news and trends.

The future of affiliate marketing holds exciting possibilities. By staying ahead of industry trends, embracing new technologies, adapting to changing consumer behavior, exploring global opportunities, and continually evolving your strategy, you can ensure your affiliate marketing business thrives in the future.

CONCLUSION

Congratulations on making it through this comprehensive guide on affiliate marketing! From understanding what affiliate marketing is to exploring future trends, you've navigated through a lot of information. Whether you're an 'Old Geezer' or a 'High School Kid,' the knowledge acquired here is the stepping stone to building a successful affiliate marketing venture.

This journey has shown us that affiliate marketing is much more than posting links and earning commissions. It's about identifying the right products, building an online presence, creating valuable content, engaging your audience, and cultivating trust. It's about testing, learning, and adapting. It's about understanding your audience, whether seniors or high school students, and meeting their unique needs. It's about complying with laws and regulations, dealing with challenges, and constantly evolving to stay ahead in this dynamic industry.

Remember, success in affiliate marketing doesn't come overnight. It requires patience, persistence, and hard work.

But with the right approach and mindset, the rewards can be substantial. As you venture into the world of affiliate marketing, remember the key takeaways from each chapter. Apply the strategies, tools, and tips shared in this guide. Stay ethical and transparent in your dealings. Continually learn, experiment, and optimize your strategies.

As the industry continues to evolve, so should your knowledge and strategies. Stay updated with the latest trends, adapt to changing consumer behaviors, and don't be afraid to innovate and try new approaches. Affiliate marketing is an exciting journey filled with challenges and opportunities. Embrace it, learn from it, and most importantly, enjoy it. Here's to your success in the world of affiliate marketing! Thank you for joining us on this journey. May the road ahead be filled with success and prosperity.

<-END->

www.ingramcontent.com/pod-product-compliance
Lightning Source LLC
Chambersburg PA
CBHW060845260726

48661CB00002B/617